After Dark

Lyanne Wang

BookLeaf
Publishing

India | USA | UK

Presentation by *BookLeaf Publishing*

Web: www.bookleafpub.com

E-mail: info@bookleafpub.com

ISBN: 9789358312478

First edition 2023

For Natalie, as always

PREFACE

In April of 2022 I experienced true loss for the first time. Looking back, I see that month as a color: as a deep blue clouded in black. It is this vision that inspired the title and first poem of this book: *After Dark*.

The immediate and overbearing darkness of grief had swallowed me, and I turned to writing to pour this murk out onto paper. The first poems of *After Dark* trace back to that time, when I was alone with the lamp turned off, transcribing my aches into a notebook.

Soon, however, I discovered it was reading that could pour light into me. It was the words of distant authors that held me firm. Poems from hundreds of years ago recounted the same pain I felt, and not only that, recounted the relieving of such pain. I draw heavy inspiration from Mary Oliver, Robert Frost, and Sylvia Plath in their ability to consolidate both sadness and joy into reality.

As months carried on, I recorded my thoughts on loss each time my emotions grew large. These thoughts now appear in this book in a mostly chronological order; in many ways, this book is a diary. I strung together 21 poems to portray my experience with grief as it happened and as it is happening. However, I hope that the speaker of each piece is read in their own context and that, when read together, the poems voice a collective experience of change.

I write this as an 18-year-old, knowing that I am inconstant, evolving each day. This book stamps my growth from April of 2022 up until this moment: it holds my love and grief simultaneously. It magnifies my evolution of *feeling,* and it chronicles my memories into permanence.

Someone once told me to open myself up to others, and I have always hoped to do so through literature. Thank you for reading.

After dark

After dark
there is blue. I sleep into the sea and the hue
presses between my breaths.
It fills my chest—
I store the treasure that sinks
me. There is a pounding
heart at the ocean floor.

After dark, blue is infinite and more.

Secrets / Storm

You and I play wisteria and foxglove
In another world we are together, entangled in an
absent plot,
Meek with secrets
Unsaid but digested
We are the choice
To kiss away sins
Hiding darkness within mouths,
Swallowing shame like soiled streams
Chewing up structure and upturning homes
Crossing neighborhoods without names—
The ones where light and deep twist into black,
We are love protruding from the ground.

The casket is enclosed

The casket is enclosed
in a bubble, and I am pressing my sadness against the stone.
Gray outlines splatter on the concrete
Where rocks and flowers come as one.
Curves are no different from lines in this dimension
That crams Earth between fire and water.
Mothers and daughters clasp fingers to touch
A piece of their past and future.
I watch from beyond the horizon
Tangent to the sun and rainbow.
You and I exist in the same plane
Made not of flesh but of air.

There is a knife in my stomach

There is a knife in my stomach
Or perhaps it's a rock
I would surely like to vomit
But I know that it'd linger, and I'd empty myself
Of only dirt and twigs

Maybe I'll down a cup
To wear its edges away
Erode the fist until its bones prod at my skin
It'll simply sink, however,
Piling as debris in my ankles

I'll go for a swim
To knock it all out
But I won't stay afloat
Despite the air in my lungs
I cannot breathe, and I cannot plunge

I will only lie there, sideways
Growing used to the ache
Until it doesn't pulse and doesn't poke
It just sits, hungry,
And heavy.

I method act to achieve perfection

I method act to achieve perfection
I do not stop until it's right
Everything I do is
Measured precise
And yet
I sigh—

Absolution

There is something stuck to my hands,
a stickiness eager to stay.
It roams and spreads around my legs,
Pressing me where I cannot see.

I scrub my skin and pray to God,
"Never again. Promise. Promise."
My heart thumps twice, the silence clear,
The lone response my heavy head.

I sulk and squirm, the water's warm.
It is me. It is me.
The liquid coats my skin and soul,
I am the filth. I am the filth.

Step out the bath and wear clean clothes,
Rid all my grime on the white towel,
Never again. Promise. Promise.
But I know. It is me. It is me.

I look back with a dagger in hand

I look back with a dagger in hand,
Would I kill if I could?
Spring is the voice that commands,
A jolt that bursts like roots of the Woods.

It is dark and I cannot see,
But I will find my way,
For though the winter dusk hides name, face, and body,
I have rage greater than May.

Words hold me like the arm of a mother

Words hold me like the arm of a mother.
The ancient twists and turns of a lone wrist
brand deeper than the notes I copy time
and time again. There are thoughts in those shapes
that persist without form, holding secrets
and wounds, ardor and aches, wishes and wants.
I pull and I tug for solace in space.
For stupor in commas, and answers in
Letters. I pour myself to them, and they
hold me sure: upright, firm, and full of thought.

I want

I want to hold the hand of the child that sits in your
stomach.

I want to hold her with more care than how I touch
you now,

with enough tenderness I could kill,

my fingers potent with comfort.

I want to hold your waist and press my ear against
your abdomen,

I'll listen to the calls, I'll feel for the quakes
I'll reach and hold your clenched fists.

My greatest wish is that I am here for you and that I
always have been;
But the truth is that I am here for you, and I always
will be.

Rain

There's a certain scent to the air
That hangs beneath my lips
When leaves begin to droop
Not with fright but with a sigh

I'd like to lie down
For a minute or a few
Just to smell the soft breeze
Of the dirt on the floor

I'll sink for a moment
Beneath the weight of the dew
Lose sight of the sky
And forget of the stars

But then water will fall
And kiss my cheek gently
Whispering back words of sempiternity
In her stream of catharsis

That washes the Earth
From the sky to my skin
Soaking perpetuity
In her lingering petrichor

You, first

Sneak through the river
As my soles sink beneath the ground
The sky is a dim blue
Just as pale as the water
That laps by our ankles
I'll catch up, sooner or later
When the waves part
And you've made it across
You, first

Mortality

I am weightless,
Tiptoeing
Across the sky,
Glancing down, only now and then,
Admiring
How the traffic ebbs and flows,
Yet never halts

Unlike the bird
That cuts through the wind,
Brilliantly quick,
But dependent on descent,
To muster enough energy
To fly again
Weightless, across the sky.

Waiting with silence

In between the slashes of pine and bark
is a pool of light
where I lay and listen for you.
Children of the sun reach to brush my chin. Fingers
tap my cheeks, my eyes, my hair.
Here, flowers never wilt, never wish to.
Nothing passes—whispers
of your name float above me like dust of a ray,
drifting as slow as warmth,
kissing the rim of my skin.
Here, above the soft pad of defeated twigs, I am still.
Here, there is stasis in the afternoon golden.
There is peace in waiting with silence.

The Size of Anger

My anger is slow burning
        I understand.
because I understand, I do, and I know you well enough to
know that you *had to;*
        I understand.
And I know you well enough to know that you would, but
        I understand.
as much as I say I know you I know that I do not know
        I understand.
all the things that I do now because if I did I would be
infinite, I would contain the multitudes
        I understand.
I thought I read and knew;
        I understand.
Yes, it turns out I am a newborn star
        I understand.
exploding and swallowing simultaneously,
        I understand.
the way my anger pulses between small and medium.

I know Frost better than I know you

I know Frost better than I know you.
His words, his wisdom, resound in my room,
I hear them with my eyes closed,
His deep voice more familiar than yours.

I know *you* like I know the cold
An old ache that hugs me tight
That melts without permission
I know *you* like I know everyone real
You're more major and fleeting than anything else.

Dependence

My father loves to fish, and I, to love him, sit close
by and watch.
It is that terrible hour now: the sun casts a dull coat of
quiet, and I have too much time to think.
The dark blurs of young fish make my heart twinge—
How stupid, how naive must they be?
Their terrible eyes and deep hunger so eagerly
deceive them to death.
Slosh! That's it!
They flop their tails between my father's fat fingers,
desperately expanding, then shrinking, as their captor
grows taller, prouder.
My father turns to me, gripping the animal's mouth
with his thumb and pointer finger. He grins. I smile.
I wonder, do I depend on the fish like air?

If you must die

If you must die
I'll envy the dirt that holds you still
I'll scoop the earth, handful by handful
Until I sit in a trench of mud

If you must die
I'll whisper to the sky
And hum to the birds
And maybe, I'll catch a glimpse of something you've
touched

If you must die
I'll lie in plains of grass
To watch the clouds pass
One by one

If you must die
I'll curse the earth that touches your skin
For hugging your death before mine
For holding you longer than I

But if you must die
As I know that you do
I think I will thank this earth
For allowing my life have began with you

I am small, but I am whole

I am small, but I am whole,
And I grow, like plants in soil,
with sun and water,
I am thankful for my father and mother,
For them I breathe, and I stand, tall.
There is much to reach for; I forget my hands are small.
I'll grab handful by handful,
Burn my shadows until they boil,
Just to soar into the sky,
And call my life mine.

The Wishbone

There is a bone that splits at my reach;
If I think too hard I might find it and break it
so I turn, left, I go around
and breach the past and future, there is a
branch to grab and I want
to swing like my
ancestors in light of
the major explosion.
I'm in my head, the
world is young and small.
I dangle at the tip of seventy stems, dripping and sweet.
Please
do not fall, the fruit
that's rich with you and a story. Right,
I do not wish to grow old with contempt and empty
palms,
I recede like swells as the
weather grows cold—or when I simply do—as death
and rebirth squeeze me thin. Brittle feathers drift off a
batting
wing to collect joy in a child's hair.
Space extends beyond my fingertips because I am
composed of a billion
years. Left and right, gravity exists, and I am true.
Bring me down to Earth without the burden of promise
but with the
naïvety of a bug, and I swear, I swear—
I feel it all in me, I am dizzy:
There exists a newborn and a song below the bird's
neck and above the breast. This time is ripe:
I might just eat it all!

Duty

Who am I,
but to live dutifully
and die gracefully
without a pinch of anger
in this big, great world.

After dark

After dark
there is blue. I sleep into the sky and the hue
Presses between my breaths.
It fills my chest—
I store the treasure that sinks
me. There is a pounding
heart in me.

After dark, let it be.